Happy Friday All

TC Duphorn

I would like to give thanks to:

Daniel Zehnder, E.H. Night (Author) for
helping me format this book,
JD Parsons (Editor and Author) for
helping me edit this book,
Roxana Renaud for cover art.

And all my friends and family
for your support.

1.

Happy Friday All.

Also, happy first week of the new year.
You have made it through the first week.
I hope, this new year is bringing you all
that you deserve and so much more.
Remember,
tomorrow is not promised to you and,
most of all, remember who you are.
With each passing day,
it is your choice to do what you want to do
or be who you want to be.

**I love you all,
and have an awesome
weekend.**

2.

Happy Friday All.

Do not let anyone take the light out of your eyes, steal your soul, or leave you empty. You are strong, wise, and beautiful in every way. Keep your light shining.

I love you all, and have an awesome weekend.

3.

Happy Friday All.

It's not about the mistakes you make,
but the willingness to make amends.
Being mindful of the people around you is
the best gift you can give yourself.
When you truly treat people like you want
to be treated, that is the greatest reward.

I love you all,
and have an awesome
weekend.

4.

Happy Friday All.

I woke up one day in love.
I wanted to give love.
Not everybody wants to receive it.
Not everyone wants to accept you as you
are. Be bold and be you.
Be ready to receive love and give love.

I love you all,
and have an awesome
weekend.

5.

Happy Friday All.

Today is the day to be exceptional.
Today is your day to shine,
your time to be lifted up.
Today is your time to grow.
You made it through the week and now
it's time to enjoy the weekend.

I love you all,
and have an awesome
weekend.

6.

Happy Friday All.

Sometimes if you're really lucky,
you meet people to help you grow.
I am ready to grow and ready to find
myself again.
It is scary, but if you have great friends
behind you, you will be okay.

**I love you all,
and have an awesome
weekend.**

7.

Happy Friday All.

Ask, believe, and achieve. If you really
want to change things in your life,
get rid of the negative and bring in the
positive; it all starts with you.
It is easy to complain; we all do it.
It is hard to do something about it.
When you dare to step out of the box,
you might step on a few cracks,
but you're also breaking the chains to
your freedom.

**I love you all,
and have an awesome
weekend.**

8.

Happy Friday All.

When you give up control,
you have a lot more fun.
I often try to control every situation,
but I'm working on letting go every day.
What I've noticed is, when I let go and
give up total control, not only do I have a
great time, but I'm at peace as well.
Let go a little. Smell the roses. Throw
caution to the wind sometimes and live.

I love you all, and have an awesome weekend.

9.

Happy Friday All.

Remember, it is totally okay to do what is best for you, to be who you want to be. It is better to tell the truth and be hated than to lie and be loved, because when you look in the mirror, you have to live with yourself.

**I love you all,
and have an awesome
weekend.**

10.

Happy Friday All.

You are the very best you can be.
You are beauty.
You are strong, wise, and beautiful.
Don't you ever forget that.
Do your best every day and make the sun
shine through the clouds.
Don't ever change.

I love you all,
and have an awesome
weekend.

11.

Happy Friday All.

I love the days,
when everything works out right,
when we can talk about problems but not
let them take over our lives,
when we can lift each other up and
inspire each other without any
expectations whatsoever,
when we can leave a conversation,
feeling better than when we arrived and
with a feeling like we learned something.
Be inspired. Be great. Be loved.

**I love you all,
and have an awesome
weekend.**

12.

When you go on your journey through life, everyone you meet along the way is not meant to be beside you.
Some are there for guidance.
Some are there for lessons.
Some are there for heartbreak.
Some are there for strength.
It is your road alone to travel through.
Choose wisely.

I love you all, and have an awesome weekend.

13.

Happy Friday All.

We all have a purpose in this life.
Sometimes, it seems like we will never
truly figure out why we are here,
but I assure you that you will realize your
talents and rise to the occasion.

I love you all,
and have an awesome
weekend.

14.

Happy Friday All.

When you listen, you hear.
When you look, you see.
When you don't try to be anything else
but you, you're golden.

**I love you all,
and have an awesome
weekend.**

15.

Happy Friday All.

It takes more than hard work and determination for success. It takes drive, the ability to never give up and to learn from your mistakes.
You can't do the same thing and expect a different result. But you can bend the road and find your passion.

I love you all, and have an awesome weekend.

16.

Happy Friday All.

Wow, what a week.
We have survived.
We have lived to fight another day.
I'll say this again, folks:
Do not let hate, anger,
and jealousy run your life.
Each day we wake up is a blessing.
Hug more, love more, and live more.
Do not let anyone make you feel small.
Picture this and warm hugs from me to
you just because you're you.

I love you all, and have an awesome weekend.

17.

Ever wonder if you're the only sane
person in the room?
In the town? In the city? In the world?
I wonder every day.
At the end of the day,
there is always a new day.
A new time for smiles and adventures,
for love and laughter...
Let the new day begin.

I love you all,
and have an awesome
weekend.

18.

Happy Friday All.

You don't have to be afraid to love.
Give it up. Do not be scared to tell people
your feelings. Shout out.
Dance when no one's watching.
Even if they are watching,
it's okay to lose control.
Just breathe and live.

I love you all,
and have an awesome
weekend.

19.

When we think about how we treat people, are we doing our very best?
When we say "Hello" and "How are you doing?", do we really mean it?
When we smile at a person, is it sincere?
Do we even look each other in the eyes anymore?
Or are we so filled up with Facebook, Snapchat, and Twitter that we forget to live life and be kind and talk in person?
Are you living through social media, or are you living?

I love you all,
and have an awesome weekend.

20.

Life is full of changes.
Some we are ready for; others we are blindsided by.
The key to true survival is to always be ready for change. Be scared but able to jump into the unknown.
The ability to survive and conquer our demons is an ongoing day-to-day process.
Not fighting is giving up.

**I love you all,
and have an awesome
weekend.**

21.

Happy Friday All.

You only get what you give.
Give kindness, give compassion,
give acceptance, give wisdom.
Lend a hand.
Be the best you can be without excuses,
without expectations.
Just be your true self.

**I love you all,
and have an awesome
weekend.**

22.

Happy Friday All.

Sometimes the best thing you can do for you is relax. You see everything that is going on, and you don't have to change it. Sometimes it's okay to let go, rewind, regroup, and rebuild.
We cannot be at one hundred percent every day. We need downtime.
It's so nice to know that you can make yourself better and the world did not fall apart.

I love you all, and have an awesome weekend.

23.

Happy Friday All.

Give yourself a big hug. You have made it
through the week.
We tend to often be too wrapped up in
our own problems to see that life is
waiting for us.
Let's go...
Dust yourself off and start all over again.
There are so many things we could do in
life to enjoy life.
I'll be your shoulder. Climb that hill...
I'm right behind you.

**I love you all,
and have an awesome
weekend.**

24.

Happy Friday All.

Sometimes people come into your life so that you can grow.
Sometimes you think you are teaching someone and you end up learning more than you teach.
The key is to allow yourself to be open, and even if the other person is not, you will still be able to learn and grow.

I love you all, and have an awesome weekend.

25.

Happy Friday All.

The courage to forgive and pay it forward is rewarding. We must love with our whole heart, give with everything we have, strive to be the best we can be in whatever we do, and just enjoy life.
It is not our burden to take on another person's hate problems or unwillingness to grow. It takes more energy to hate and to be spiteful than it does to love without judgment.

I love you all, and have an awesome weekend.

26.

Happy Friday All.

The past can set you free if you let it.
You cannot just let it dig up old bones
that can drive you insane.
Forgive yourself.
Remember the good times.
Learn from the bad.
Move forward.

I love you all,
and have an awesome
weekend.

27.

Happy Friday All.

Happiness is a state of mind.
When you think of it that way it will help
you get your happy back.
I choose to be happy and love today.
I choose to give freely and expect nothing
in return.

**I love you all,
and have an awesome
weekend.**

28.

Happy Friday All.

The most important job you will ever have
is working on yourself.
We do not get to run and hide.
It follows us.
We do not get to move on with different
people.
The problems always follow.
We have to love ourselves and be kind in
order to be better and do better.
We have to learn how to like and love
ourselves so that our problems never
follow.

I love you all,
and have an awesome
weekend.

29.

Happy Friday All.

We are not all made for each other.
There are people that love to judge and
think they are better than the rest.
Let them judge.
We are too busy living our best lives.

I love you all,
and have an awesome
weekend.

30.

Sometimes it is okay to step away from
the train wreck. No one is perfect;
this I know too much about.
But I have noticed, that people often
make a lot of excuses for bad behavior
and bad decisions.
If you don't want to be judged,
stop doing stupid stuff.
Take responsibility for your life and the
people around you.
Do your best every day and if you fall
down, get back up.
Do not be a victim of negativity or bad
thoughts.
Do better and be better.

**I love you all,
and have an awesome
weekend.**

31.

Happy Friday All.

This week has been full of finding out new things about me.
Sometimes we forget, what it is like to be free... Like we were as children.
Dreaming and living for each day not worrying about things that might happen or what could have been.
When you reach inside what do you see?
I see a little girl wanting to save the world with smiles and hugs and lots of love...
What do you see?

**I love you all,
and have an awesome
weekend.**

32.

This week I have learned one valuable
thing.
The road you travel.
Some people are meant to be in your life
for a moment, to give you joy or love
make you feel good.
Some people grow with you and it is a
wonderful journey.
Some people fade away... That makes me
sad when people fade away.
But remember it is the road you travel not
theirs that determines your self-worth.
Stay focused never surround yourself with
takers and give back because you can.

I love you all,
and have an awesome
weekend.

33.

What makes a man?
Is it the mistakes you make?
Is it the chances you take?
Is it failure?
Is it failure to not try at all?
Is it the ability to never give up?
Is it the strength to keep on going?
Or the strength to walk away?
Sometimes the answers are right in front of you.
Sometimes there are no answers.
Sometimes we just have to be and let it be.

**I love you all,
and have an awesome
weekend.**

34.

Happy Friday All.

Today is a good day. I just want to say to you all that we are lucky to have everything that we have.
We do not live in a perfect world, but if we open our hearts and minds then we will make it a better world.
Love each other and treat each other with respect.
We do not have all the answers, but let's make a better tomorrow...

I love you all, and have an awesome weekend.

35.

Happy Friday All.

When the light hits your eyes,
always remember to shine.

**I love you all,
and have an awesome
weekend.**

36.

Happy Friday All.

Ever think you're walking the same road
with nowhere in sight?
Stop, look around,
see a different path, and take it.
The road you travel is never light,
but filled with adventures.

**I love you all,
and have an awesome
weekend.**

37.

Happy Friday All.

Wow, I have learned a lot this week.
Forgiveness and kindness are key.
It is ok to be sad mad and angry but you
cannot allow that to cloud your heart.
Someone once told me it is not black or
white but gray and when the sun rises we
must choose to smile and be happy and I
choose to be happy.

I love you all,
and have an awesome
weekend.

38.

People will often disappoint you,
but people can often make you believe in
the goodness of man.
Do not forget to be your best self,
to help people,
and to give a smile when needed.
We are responsible for the welfare of all
mankind.

I love you all,
and have an awesome
weekend.

39.

Happy Friday All.

If we cannot appreciate the good,
there will be no good.
If we cannot give, we cannot receive.
If we cannot love, we cannot receive love.
And if we cannot be positive,
we cannot receive positivity.

**I love you all,
and have an awesome
weekend.**

40.

We all are judgmental,
but that is not an excuse to be mean or
belittle people.
I often put myself in someone else's shoes
so that I can gain a better understanding
and be more compassionate,
and I would hope,
the other person does the same.
But sometimes people are just selfish.
When we only think of ourselves and not
the other person, does that make us less
human? Does that block our blessings?
I believe in honor, respect, and kindness;
do you?

I love you all,
and have an awesome
weekend.

41.

Happy Friday All.

You only get what you give.
Give kindness, give compassion,
give acceptance, give wisdom.
Lend a hand. Be the best you can be
without excuses, without expectations.
Just be your true self.

**I love you all,
and have an awesome
weekend.**

42.

Happy Friday All.

All that you have is all that you need.
You do not have to talk to someone every
day or see them every day to know who
your real friends are.
Real friends love you for who you are and
always tell you the truth.
Real friends stand with you and make you
feel at ease.
Real friends are family.

I love you all,
and have an awesome
weekend.

43.

Happy Friday All.

Don't let anyone make you feel small.
Don't ever doubt yourself.
You have the key.
You are a bright shiny diamond.

**I love you all,
and have an awesome
weekend.**

44.

Sometimes it is ok to be sad.
If we never had lows we would never
appreciate the highs.
Just remember that in the darkest hour
there is light.
See it and be it...
It will get you through.
I will show you the way.

**I love you all,
and have an awesome
weekend.**

45.

Happy Friday All.

The most important relationship you have
is with you. When you love yourself and
treat yourself as well as you treat others
you feel like you have done your daily
best. When you feel your best you are
your best self.

I love you all,
and have an awesome
weekend.

46.

Happy Friday All.

Sometimes you need to dance in the rain.
Sometimes you need to feel the fresh air,
Sometimes you need to throw snowballs,
Living is worth living when you get the
job done.
Live hard and love hard...

I love you all,
and have an awesome
weekend.

47.

Happy Friday All.

Some people have nothing but hate in
their hearts.
Sometimes we think we can save them.
We cannot.
They have to save themselves like
everyone else.
The only thing we can do is put out the
energy we wish to receive.
Surround yourself with good people.
Be there for them and let them be there
for you.
You deserve the best.
Never settle.

I love you all,
and have an awesome
weekend.

48.

As we go into the weekend,
remember this:
Chains can bind you to sadness.
Chains can hold you back.
When we release the pain and sadness
and fear in our hearts,
we become free.
When we dare to be different,
we are free.
When we walk our own path,
we live the dream.
You are the only person that can hold
yourself back.
Let it go.

**I love you all,
and have an awesome
weekend.**

49.

Happy Friday All.

It is OK to take care of yourself.
Did you hear me?
Say it with me:
If you don't, no one else will.
It is OK for you to come first.
You will always be number 1 in my book.
It is selfish not to.

**I love you all,
and have an awesome
weekend.**

50.

Happy Friday All.

As we roll on into the weekend, remember this: The seasons are changing and people are changing.
Just open your heart and make sure you love with no judgment.
Open your heart and mind to new adventures.
Take a chance.

I love you all, and have an awesome weekend.

51.

Happy Friday All.

As the holidays draw near,
let's remember to not just be nice around
the holidays, but every day.
Let's not just give gifts,
but give love as well.
Let's acknowledge people in our lives all
the time. Not just part-time.
Give love and lots of hugs...

**I love you all,
and have an awesome
weekend.**

52.

You can't choose your family,
but you can choose your friends.
Sometimes,
you have to have a breakdown
to have a breakthrough.
And it feels so good
to have a breakthrough.

I'm wishing everyone a happy new year.

Remember to let go of all the pain before
the New Year and start fresh.
Make a plan for the New Year and stick to
it and enjoy the miracles...

**I love you all,
and have an awesome
weekend.**

About The Author:

T.C. Duphorn has been writing Happy Friday for 13 years and 2 years ago decided to make it into a book. She started this to uplift and inspire others. In Addition to writing, T.C. Duphorn enjoys cooking. She is a private chef, does catering and loves to play and write music.